Author's Journal

Journal of Author

_____

If found please return to:

_____

_____

Created by
Sleepless Psyche Publishing

A SLEEPLESSPSYCHE JOURNAL

Author's Journal

Sleepless Psyche Publishing

www.sleeplesspsyche.co.uk

Email: sleeplesspsyche@aol.com

Text Copyright © 2017 SleeplessPsyche Publishing

Illustrations © 2017 Tessa Thompson

All Rights Reserved

Contents

How to use this book	1
Story Ideas	2
Story Notes	3
Characters	23
Character Outlines	24
Plotting	45
Obligatory Scenes	46
Thrillers/Crime	46
Horror	47
Sci-Fi & Fantasy	48
Romance	49
Book Outline	50
Chapter Outlines	52
Locations (Settings)	97
Book Research Notes	122
Editing	155
Plot	155
Character	156
Setting	157
Dialogue	158
Point of View	159
Conflict	160
Golden Nuggets	161

How to use this book.

Much more than a journal for your writing, this notebook is the ultimate tool , providing you, the author, with everything you require to plan and create your novel.

From detailing the obligatory scenes of key genres, to explaining the fundamentals of character creation and outlining, this book has hints and tips for every stage in writing your novel. There are journal templates for each step in your planning, quirky illustrations and inspiring quotes.

> "A goal without a plan is just a wish..."
> Antoine de Saint-Exupere

Story Ideas

Inspiration can strike at any time – so take this book with you wherever you go and keep it on hand while you sleep.

This section is right at the front of your journal so that you can jot down any ideas that come to you. Don't worry about being neat – just get something down on paper.

> "The best time for planning your books is while you are doing the dishes"
>
> Agatha Christie

Story Ideas

Story Ideas

Story Ideas

What if?

What if?

Story Ideas

Story Ideas

Story Ideas

What if?

What if?

Story Ideas

Story Ideas

Story Ideas

Story Ideas

Story Ideas

Story Ideas

Story Ideas

Story Ideas

Story Ideas

Story Ideas

What if?

What if?

Characters

The most important thing in any book is the quality of the characters and in particular the quality of the protagonist – particularly in thrillers.

Creating high quality characters is mainly about knowing them. If you think of your characters as real people then you will write them well. So use the real people you know as the basis of your characters then...

- Give them a fault.
- Give them a purpose – something that drives them.
- Get them up into a tree (figuratively speaking).
- Throw rocks at them.
- Get them down again.

> "When writing a novel a writer should create living people; People, not characters. A character is a caricature"
> Earnest Hemmingway

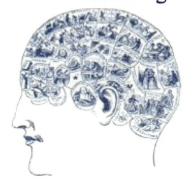

CHARACTER OUTLINE

Character Name :

Inspired by:

Character arc - Start:

Character arc - End:

Occupation/Role:

Drive/Purpose:

Manner/Attitude:

Fault/s:

Virtue/s:

Fears:

Description/Traits:

Character Outline

Character Name :

Inspired by:

Character arc - Start:

Character arc - End:

Occupation/Role:

Drive/Purpose:

Manner/Attitude:

Fault/s:

Virtue/s:

Fears:

Description/Traits:

Character Outline

Character Name :

Inspired by:

Character arc - Start:

Character arc - End:

Occupation/Role:

Drive/Purpose:

Manner/Attitude:

Fault/s:

Virtue/s:

Fears:

Description/Traits:

Character Outline

Character Name :

Inspired by:

Character arc - Start:

Character arc - End:

Occupation/Role:

Drive/Purpose:

Manner/Attitude:

Fault/s:

Virtue/s:

Fears:

Description/Traits:

Character Outline

Character Name :

Inspired by:

Character arc - Start:

Character arc - End:

Occupation/Role:

Drive/Purpose:

Manner/Attitude:

Fault/s:

Virtue/s:

Fears:

Description/Traits:

Character Outline

Character Name :

Inspired by:

Character arc - Start:

Character arc - End:

Occupation/Role:

Drive/Purpose:

Manner/Attitude:

Fault/s:

Virtue/s:

Fears:

Description/Traits:

CHARACTER OUTLINE

Character Name :

Inspired by:

Character arc - Start:

Character arc - End:

Occupation/Role:

Drive/Purpose:

Manner/Attitude:

Fault/s:

Virtue/s:

Fears:

Description/Traits:

Character Outline

Character Name :

Inspired by:

Character arc - Start:

Character arc - End:

Occupation/Role:

Drive/Purpose:

Manner/Attitude:

Fault/s:

Virtue/s:

Fears:

Description/Traits:

CHARACTER OUTLINE

Character Name :

Inspired by:

Character arc - Start:

Character arc - End:

Occupation/Role:

Drive/Purpose:

Manner/Attitude:

Fault/s:

Virtue/s:

Fears:

Description/Traits:

CHARACTER OUTLINE

Character Name :

Inspired by:

Character arc - Start:

Character arc - End:

Occupation/Role:

Drive/Purpose:

Manner/Attitude:

Fault/s:

Virtue/s:

Fears:

Description/Traits:

CHARACTER OUTLINE

Character Name :

Inspired by:

Character arc - Start:

Character arc - End:

Occupation/Role:

Drive/Purpose:

Manner/Attitude:

Fault/s:

Virtue/s:

Fears:

Description/Traits:

Character Outline

Character Name :

Inspired by:

Character arc - Start:

Character arc - End:

Occupation/Role:

Drive/Purpose:

Manner/Attitude:

Fault/s:

Virtue/s:

Fears:

Description/Traits:

Character Outline

Character Name :

Inspired by:

Character arc - Start:

Character arc - End:

Occupation/Role:

Drive/Purpose:

Manner/Attitude:

Fault/s:

Virtue/s:

Fears:

Description/Traits:

Character Outline

Character Name :

Inspired by:

Character arc - Start:

Character arc - End:

Occupation/Role:

Drive/Purpose:

Manner/Attitude:

Fault/s:

Virtue/s:

Fears:

Description/Traits:

Character Outline

Character Name:

Inspired by:

Character arc - Start:

Character arc - End:

Occupation/Role:

Drive/Purpose:

Manner/Attitude:

Fault/s:

Virtue/s:

Fears:

Description/Traits:

Character Outline

Character Name:

Inspired by:

Character arc - Start:

Character arc - End:

Occupation/Role:

Drive/Purpose:

Manner/Attitude:

Fault/s:

Virtue/s:

Fears:

Description/Traits:

CHARACTER OUTLINE

Character Name :

Inspired by:

Character arc - Start:

Character arc - End:

Occupation/Role:

Drive/Purpose:

Manner/Attitude:

Fault/s:

Virtue/s:

Fears:

Description/Traits:

Character Outline

Character Name :

Inspired by:

Character arc - Start:

Character arc - End:

Occupation/Role:

Drive/Purpose:

Manner/Attitude:

Fault/s:

Virtue/s:

Fears:

Description/Traits:

Character Outline

Character Name :

Inspired by:

Character arc - Start:

Character arc - End:

Occupation/Role:

Drive/Purpose:

Manner/Attitude:

Fault/s:

Virtue/s:

Fears:

Description/Traits:

Character Outline

Character Name :

Inspired by:

Character arc - Start:

Character arc - End:

Occupation/Role:

Drive/Purpose:

Manner/Attitude:

Fault/s:

Virtue/s:

Fears:

Description/Traits:

CHARACTER OUTLINE

Character Name :

Inspired by:

Character arc - Start:

Character arc - End:

Occupation/Role:

Drive/Purpose:

Manner/Attitude:

Fault/s:

Virtue/s:

Fears:

Description/Traits:

Plotting

The first most important thing to remember when plotting your story is that all plots have a very simple structure – like this:

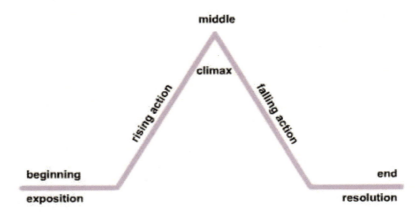

This structure is the same for the book over all *and* every chapter or scene.

The second most important thing is CONFLICT. Every scene in your book should have it. Conflict is what hooks your readers in at the start and keeps them turning the pages.

The third thing to remember is that the situation at the start of your book, chapter, or scene must be different from the situation at the end. A protagonist may be happy at the beginning but will be sad by the end or rich in the first chapter and broke in the last.

Obligatory Scenes

When plotting your book you must take into account the fact that any given genre has certain obligatory scenes. These are the conventions or tropes that the readers expect to find when reading that genre of fiction.

Here are the obligatory scenes for the most popular genres.

MYSTERY/CRIME

- **The Crime:-** A crime is committed – murder's or kidnapping are the most common. The Crime should occur early in the story as it is a great area of conflict and therefore a hook.
- **A Criminal Mastermind :-** The villain/antagonist must be intelligent enough to have hidden his identity sufficiently that it is not obvious from the beginning of your book who committed the crime.
- **The Detective/Investigator :-** He/she must be intelligent enough to solve the puzzle. Usually, if not a police officer, the protagonist has some special skill or interest that enables them to uncover clues that others may miss.

- **Now it is personal :-** At some point in the story, the protagonist, his family or friends become a victim of the villain.
- **Clues :-** The reader will expect there to be clues that if they are very smart will enable them to solve the crime. However, there should be red herrings so generally they are unable to do so until close to the end of the book.
- **The Reveal :-** The protagonist confronts / uncovers / arrests the criminal.
- **Justice is Served? :-** The ending results in justice, though sometimes, injustice or ironic justice.

HORROR

- **A fate worse than death :-** Something worth more than life itself is at stake, such as torture or eternal damnation.
- **Monster :-** The antagonist is more powerful than the hero, perhaps even supernatural.
- **All praise to the evil one :-** At the beginning of the book someone points out how powerful and evil the villain is.
- **Hero –v- Monster** confrontation :- At some point in the book, close to the climax, the hero is at the mercy of the villain.
- **False ending :-** The monster seems to have been defeated, but returns to be defeated a second and final time.

NB. Thrillers have a combination of Crime and Horror Obligatory scenes.

SCIENCE FICTION/FANTASY

- **We're not in Kansas anymore:** – We are taken to a different world / dimension where normal rules don't exist and magic or technology reign.
- **Universe Rules:** – The laws of the magical world, it's magic or technology are outlined in detail.
- **Magic/Technology has its price:** – The limitations and consequences of using the magic/technology are explained.
- **Magic/Technology causes conflict:** – War over, or the drive to possess the magic/technology drives the plot. (Quest plot) Drive is to possess the 'McGuffin', e.g. The ring in *Lord of the Rings*.
- **Magic/Technology wins the day:** – The protagonist triumphs by using magic or technology or by destroying it.

NB. Thrillers have a combination of Crime and Horror Obligatory scenes.

ROMANCE

- **The Cute Meet:**– The hero and heroine meet in an unusual way or during a life changing event.
- **External Conflict:**– Something or someone keeps them apart.
- **Internal Conflict:**– Internal emotions, doubts, guilt or misunderstandings keep them apart.
- **Magnetism:**– Despite this something forces the two together.
- **The First Kiss:**– They express their feelings for the first time.
- **The First Fight**– They quarrel but get over it.
- **The Betrayal**– Something happens that threatens to keep them apart forever. It seems insurmountable.
- **Love Conquers All:**– The lovers overcome the betrayal.
- **The Happily Ever After:**– Undying love is expressed – this can occur even after the tragic death of one of the couple as in *The Notebook, The Fault In Our Stars*, or *Titanic*.

NB. Thrillers have a combination of Crime and Horror Obligatory scenes.

Book Outline

One page per chapter outline.

Book Outline

Theme of Book:

Situation at the start of book:

Situation at the end of book:

Inciting Incident (What drives the story):

Outline of Book Arc:

Chapter One

Situation at the start:

Situation at the end:

Point of View:

Inciting Incident:

Setting:

Outline of Chapter Arc:

Chapter Two

Situation at the start:

Situation at the end:

Point of View:

Inciting Incident:

Setting:

Outline of Chapter Arc:

Chapter Three

Situation at the start:

Situation at the end:

Point of View:

Inciting Incident:

Setting:

Outline of Chapter Arc:

Chapter Four

Situation at the start:

Situation at the end:

Point of View:

Inciting Incident:

Setting:

Outline of Chapter Arc:

Chapter Five

Situation at the start:

Situation at the end:

Point of View:

Inciting Incident:

Setting:

Outline of Chapter Arc:

Chapter Six

Situation at the start:

Situation at the end:

Point of View:

Inciting Incident:

Setting:

Outline of Chapter Arc:

Chapter Seven

Situation at the start:

Situation at the end:

Point of View:

Inciting Incident:

Setting:

Outline of Chapter Arc:

Chapter Eight

Situation at the start:

Situation at the end:

Point of View:

Inciting Incident:

Setting:

Outline of Chapter Arc:

Chapter Nine

Situation at the start:

Situation at the end:

Point of View:

Inciting Incident:

Setting:

Outline of Chapter Arc:

Chapter Ten

Situation at the start:

Situation at the end:

Point of View:

Inciting Incident:

Setting:

Outline of Chapter Arc:

Chapter Eleven

Situation at the start:

Situation at the end:

Point of View:

Inciting Incident:

Setting:

Outline of Chapter Arc:

Chapter Twelve

Situation at the start:

Situation at the end:

Point of View:

Inciting Incident:

Setting:

Outline of Chapter Arc:

Chapter Thirteen

Situation at the start:

Situation at the end:

Point of View:

Inciting Incident:

Setting:

Outline of Chapter Arc:

Chapter Fourteen

Situation at the start:

Situation at the end:

Point of View:

Inciting Incident:

Setting:

Outline of Chapter Arc:

Chapter Fifteen

Situation at the start:

Situation at the end:

Point of View:

Inciting Incident:

Setting:

Outline of Chapter Arc:

Chapter Sixteen

Situation at the start:

Situation at the end:

Point of View:

Inciting Incident:

Setting:

Outline of Chapter Arc:

Chapter Seventeen

Situation at the start:

Situation at the end:

Point of View:

Inciting Incident:

Setting:

Outline of Chapter Arc:

Chapter Eighteen

Situation at the start:

Situation at the end:

Point of View:

Inciting Incident:

Setting:

Outline of Chapter Arc:

Chapter Nineteen

Situation at the start:

Situation at the end:

Point of View:

Inciting Incident:

Setting:

Outline of Chapter Arc:

Chapter Twenty

Situation at the start:

Situation at the end:

Point of View:

Inciting Incident:

Setting:

Outline of Chapter Arc:

Chapter Twenty-One

Situation at the start:

Situation at the end:

Point of View:

Inciting Incident:

Setting:

Outline of Chapter Arc:

Chapter Twenty-Two

Situation at the start:

Situation at the end:

Point of View:

Inciting Incident:

Setting:

Outline of Chapter Arc:

Chapter Twenty-Three

Situation at the start:

Situation at the end:

Point of View:

Inciting Incident:

Setting:

Outline of Chapter Arc:

Chapter Twenty-Four

Situation at the start:

Situation at the end:

Point of View:

Inciting Incident:

Setting:

Outline of Chapter Arc:

Chapter Twenty-Five

Situation at the start:

Situation at the end:

Point of View:

Inciting Incident:

Setting:

Outline of Chapter Arc:

Chapter Twenty-Six

Situation at the start:

Situation at the end:

Point of View:

Inciting Incident:

Setting:

Outline of Chapter Arc:

Chapter Twenty-Seven

Situation at the start:

Situation at the end:

Point of View:

Inciting Incident:

Setting:

Outline of Chapter Arc:

Chapter Twenty-Eight

Situation at the start:

Situation at the end:

Point of View:

Inciting Incident:

Setting:

Outline of Chapter Arc:

Chapter Twenty-Nine

Situation at the start:

Situation at the end:

Point of View:

Inciting Incident:

Setting:

Outline of Chapter Arc:

Chapter Thirty

Situation at the start:

Situation at the end:

Point of View:

Inciting Incident:

Setting:

Outline of Chapter Arc:

Chapter Thirty-One

Situation at the start:

Situation at the end:

Point of View:

Inciting Incident:

Setting:

Outline of Chapter Arc:

Chapter Thirty-Two

Situation at the start:

Situation at the end:

Point of View:

Inciting Incident:

Setting:

Outline of Chapter Arc:

Chapter Thirty-Three

Situation at the start:

Situation at the end:

Point of View:

Inciting Incident:

Setting:

Outline of Chapter Arc:

Chapter Thirty-Four

Situation at the start:

Situation at the end:

Point of View:

Inciting Incident:

Setting:

Outline of Chapter Arc:

Chapter Thirty-Five

Situation at the start:

Situation at the end:

Point of View:

Inciting Incident:

Setting:

Outline of Chapter Arc:

Chapter Thirty-Six

Situation at the start:

Situation at the end:

Point of View:

Inciting Incident:

Setting:

Outline of Chapter Arc:

Chapter Thirty-Seven

Situation at the start:

Situation at the end:

Point of View:

Inciting Incident:

Setting:

Outline of Chapter Arc:

Chapter Thirty-Eight

Situation at the start:

Situation at the end:

Point of View:

Inciting Incident:

Setting:

Outline of Chapter Arc:

Chapter Thirty-Nine

Situation at the start:

Situation at the end:

Point of View:

Inciting Incident:

Setting:

Outline of Chapter Arc:

Chapter Forty

Situation at the start:

Situation at the end:

Point of View:

Inciting Incident:

Setting:

Outline of Chapter Arc:

Chapter Fourty-One

Situation at the start:

Situation at the end:

Point of View:

Inciting Incident:

Setting:

Outline of Chapter Arc:

Chapter Forty-Two

Situation at the start:

Situation at the end:

Point of View:

Inciting Incident:

Setting:

Outline of Chapter Arc:

Chapter Forty-Three

Situation at the start:

Situation at the end:

Point of View:

Inciting Incident:

Setting:

Outline of Chapter Arc:

Chapter Forty-Four

Situation at the start:

Situation at the end:

Point of View:

Inciting Incident:

Setting:

Outline of Chapter Arc:

Chapter Forty-Five

Situation at the start:

Situation at the end:

Point of View:

Inciting Incident:

Setting:

Outline of Chapter Arc:

Chapter Forty-Six

Situation at the start:

Situation at the end:

Point of View:

Inciting Incident:

Setting:

Outline of Chapter Arc:

LOCATIONS

Location _____

What do you see?

What do you hear?

What do you smell?

What do you feel?

What is special about this place?

LOCATIONS

Location _____

What do you see?

What do you hear?

What do you smell?

What do you feel?

What is special about this place?

LOCATIONS

Location _____

What do you see?

What do you hear?

What do you smell?

What do you feel?

What is special about this place?

LOCATIONS

Location _____

What do you see?

What do you hear?

What do you smell?

What do you feel?

What is special about this place?

LOCATIONS

Location _____

What do you see?

What do you hear?

What do you smell?

What do you feel?

What is special about this place?

LOCATIONS

Location _____

What do you see?

What do you hear?

What do you smell?

What do you feel?

What is special about this place?

LOCATIONS

Location _____

What do you see?

What do you hear?

What do you smell?

What do you feel?

What is special about this place?

LOCATIONS

Location _____

What do you see?

What do you hear?

What do you smell?

What do you feel?

What is special about this place?

LOCATIONS

Location _____

What do you see?

What do you hear?

What do you smell?

What do you feel?

What is special about this place?

LOCATIONS

Location _____

What do you see?

What do you hear?

What do you smell?

What do you feel?

What is special about this place?

LOCATIONS

Location _____

What do you see?

What do you hear?

What do you smell?

What do you feel?

What is special about this place?

LOCATIONS

Location _____

What do you see?

What do you hear?

What do you smell?

What do you feel?

What is special about this place?

LOCATIONS

Location _____

What do you see?

What do you hear?

What do you smell?

What do you feel?

What is special about this place?

LOCATIONS

Location _____

What do you see?

What do you hear?

What do you smell?

What do you feel?

What is special about this place?

LOCATIONS

Location _____

What do you see?

What do you hear?

What do you smell?

What do you feel?

What is special about this place?

LOCATIONS

Location _____

What do you see?

What do you hear?

What do you smell?

What do you feel?

What is special about this place?

LOCATIONS

Location _____

What do you see?

What do you hear?

What do you smell?

What do you feel?

What is special about this place?

LOCATIONS

Location _____

What do you see?

What do you hear?

What do you smell?

What do you feel?

What is special about this place?

LOCATIONS

Location _____

What do you see?

What do you hear?

What do you smell?

What do you feel?

What is special about this place?

LOCATIONS

Location _____

What do you see?

What do you hear?

What do you smell?

What do you feel?

What is special about this place?

LOCATIONS

Location _____

What do you see?

What do you hear?

What do you smell?

What do you feel?

What is special about this place?

LOCATIONS

Location _____

What do you see?

What do you hear?

What do you smell?

What do you feel?

What is special about this place?

LOCATIONS

Location _____

What do you see?

What do you hear?

What do you smell?

What do you feel?

What is special about this place?

LOCATIONS

Location _____

What do you see?

What do you hear?

What do you smell?

What do you feel?

What is special about this place?

LOCATIONS

Location _____

What do you see?

What do you hear?

What do you smell?

What do you feel?

What is special about this place?

BOOK RESEARCH NOTES

BOOK RESEARCH NOTES

BOOK RESEARCH NOTES

BOOK RESEARCH NOTES

BOOK RESEARCH NOTES

BOOK RESEARCH NOTES

BOOK RESEARCH NOTES

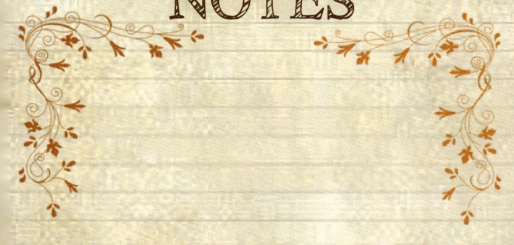

BOOK RESEARCH NOTES

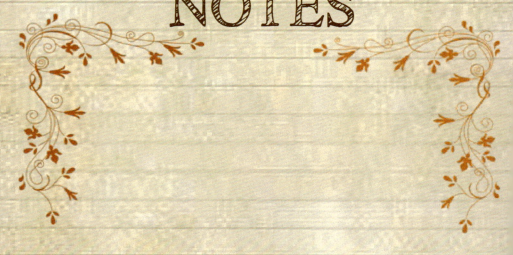

BOOK RESEARCH NOTES

BOOK RESEARCH NOTES

BOOK RESEARCH NOTES

BOOK RESEARCH NOTES

BOOK RESEARCH NOTES

BOOK RESEARCH NOTES

BOOK RESEARCH NOTES

BOOK RESEARCH NOTES

BOOK RESEARCH NOTES

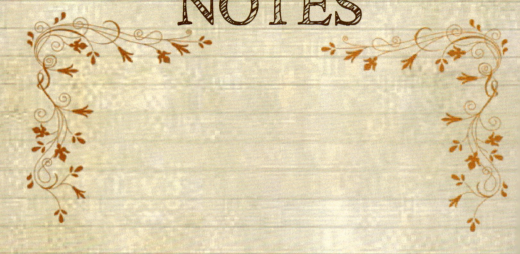

BOOK RESEARCH NOTES

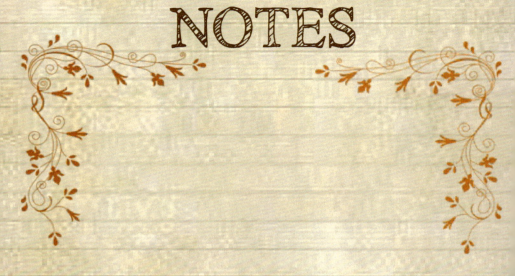

BOOK RESEARCH NOTES

BOOK RESEARCH NOTES

BOOK RESEARCH NOTES

BOOK RESEARCH NOTES

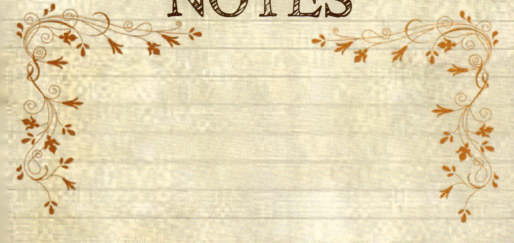

BOOK RESEARCH NOTES

BOOK RESEARCH NOTES

BOOK RESEARCH NOTES

BOOK RESEARCH NOTES

BOOK RESEARCH NOTES

BOOK RESEARCH NOTES

BOOK RESEARCH NOTES

BOOK RESEARCH NOTES

BOOK RESEARCH NOTES

BOOK RESEARCH NOTES

BOOK RESEARCH NOTES

Editing

Plot

Is it interesting and engrossing and believable?

Is there enough to sustain the story through the final page?

Are there too many sub-plots, not enough sub-plots?

Are major plot issues resolved?

Does the story start in the right place?

Dump any coincidences and make sure you....

include surprises!

Editing

Character

Are lead characters interesting enough for the story?

Do lead characters have sufficient motivation

Is the antagonist strong enough?

Do characters have strengths *and* weaknesses?

Are character goals clear?

Are characters well-rounded?

Are there any unnecessary Characters?

Do characters have appropriate and sufficient habits, quirks, favourite words, speech patterns, dreams, goals and motivations?

Make characters three-dimensional—include thoughts, actions, and reactions

Editing

Setting

Is it conveyed effectively?

Is it appropriate for the story?

Would a different setting work better?

Is setting used to advance plot, to create tone, to increase tension?

Are readers given a clear sense of place and time for each scene?

Does the setting overwhelm action or plot?

Editing

Dialogue

Does dialogue advance the story?

Is dialogue appropriate to character?

Is dialogue appropriate to the scene?

Does dialogue increase conflict?

Do the characters sound sufficiently different?

Editing

Point of view

Is it the right POV for the story and for the scene; would another be better?

Is POV clear?

Is POV maintained within scenes?

(no head-hopping)

Editing

Conflict

Is there sufficient conflict in each scene and between characters?

Does conflict escalate?

Is their sufficient tension?

Golden Nuggets

Show - do not tell
Kill the Adjectives
Drop the Clichés
Write, Write, Write
Edit, Edit, Edit
Read Dialogue Aloud
Kill your Darlings
Enjoy your Craft!

If you enjoyed this book...

Why not visit out website for information about
All our latest releases, special offers and free gifts.

http://www.sleeplesspsyche.co.uk